Trucks

Alan Thomas

Illustrated by
Michael Roffe
Rhoda and Robert Burns

A Piccolo Book

Contents

Edited by Deri Warren
Designed by David Jefferis

Designed and produced by Grisewood & Dempsey Ltd
and exclusively distributed under the
Piccolo imprint by Pan Books Ltd,
18–21 Cavaye Place, London SW10 9PG.
© Grisewood & Dempsey Ltd 1987
ISBN 0 330 29705 8
9 8 7 6 5 4 3 2 1
Phototypeset by Waveney Typesetters, Norwich
Printed and bound in Portugal by Printer Portuguesa.

Introduction

Every kind of industry is important, but the most vital one of all is transport. Without the transport industry none of the others could survive, as there would be no way of getting goods to customers. And for the last forty years, the most important kind of transport for goods has been the trucking industry.

The first motor trucks were made nearly ninety years ago. These early trucks were small and slow, and suitable only for local work such as distributing the goods carried by the railways. Then, over the years, trucks began to replace the railways for long-distance deliveries too.

The main reason that road transport has taken the place of railways (and canals, rivers and even in some cases ships), is that it is much more efficient and economical. With the other forms of transport, trucks are still needed to deliver the goods at either end. Trucks are cheaper and more convenient because once each vehicle is loaded it can travel directly to its destination. This makes it possible to organize collections and deliveries without the need for complicated timetables and formal arrangements. It also means that a continuous delivery service can be set up, so only a small quantity of goods needs to be kept in stock by the customer.

In comparison with all their competitors, trucks are cheap to buy and to maintain. Additional ones can be bought when they are needed, and sold again when there is no more work for them.

The development of vehicles and roads has gone forward together, so that as the modern motorway networks grew, trucks able to cover long distances at high speeds were built. Today, trucks make journeys covering thousands of kilometres, using special ferries to cross seaways.

GLOSSARY

Air deflector   Moulded shield mounted on cab roof. It helps to streamline a vehicle, and saves fuel.

Axle   A beam which carries a road wheel at each end. Drive axles contain transmission gearing.

Chassis   The base frame on which all the other parts of a vehicle are mounted.

Compressor unit   On refrigerated bodies, the equipment that controls the temperature.

Container transporter   Usually a semi-trailer made as a simple frame to carry container boxes.

Drawbar   The towing frame that connects a trailer to the vehicle which tows it.

Filler panels   Panelwork concealing awkward gaps, as in those under a cab when it is raised on a chassis.

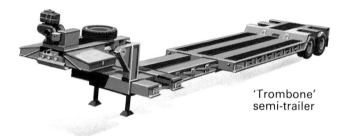

'Trombone'
semi-trailer

Semi-trailer   A trailer in which the front end, and some of the weight, is carried by a tractor.

Streamlined   A vehicle in which sharp corners and gaps are smoothed, making it easier for air to flow over it.

Swop-bodies   Interchangeable bodywork, with which one body can be loaded while the chassis is carrying another.

Tandem (usually axles)   When two axles are placed close together in order to share the weight.

Tractor   The cab and engine part of an articulated lorry. It carries some of the semi-trailer weight.

Trailer   A vehicle with no engine that is towed. It carries all its weight on its own wheels.

Triaxle   The arrangement, usually on semi-trailers, where three axles are mounted close together.

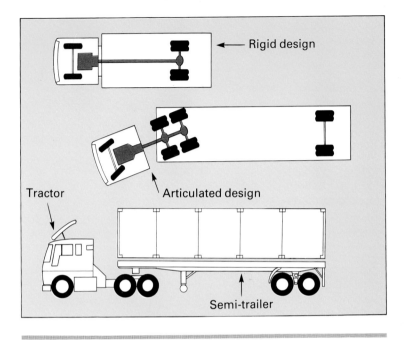

Rigid design

Tractor

Articulated design

Semi-trailer

Truck Design

There are three main kinds of truck used to carry goods –
the rigid, with two, three or four **axles**, which carries the
load on its own back; the truck and **trailer**, in which a
rigid hauls a separate four or six-wheeled vehicle which
has no engine; and the articulated. In the 'artic', a
tractor unit carries the front end of a **semi-trailer** –
'semi' because it has no road wheels of its own at the
front. An artic is far more flexible than a rigid
since it bends just behind the driver's cab, and even
a very large one can be threaded through busy streets.

In some countries, **drawbar** trailers are encouraged.
These are even more flexible on the road, and have
another big advantage: the truck and trailer can make
most of a journey as a single train, but can then be
uncoupled to make separate deliveries.

Wheels and Weights

The laws controlling road transport state that no fully-loaded truck may weigh more than the limit set for its class. Some towns and cities refuse to allow large trucks into their streets at all. There are also laws which state that each wheel and each axle may not carry more than a certain weight. When you also consider how many different types of cargo need to be carried, it is not surprising that such a variety of truck shapes, with so many different wheel arrangements, are seen on the roads today. Some of the most common designs are shown in the diagram below.

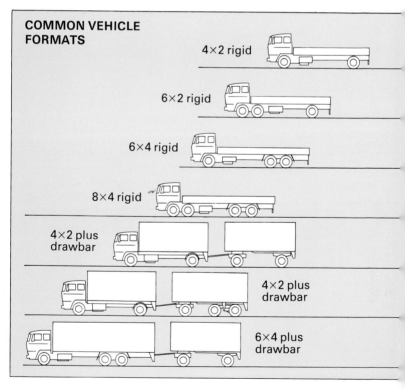

COMMON VEHICLE FORMATS

4×2 rigid

6×2 rigid

6×4 rigid

8×4 rigid

4×2 plus drawbar

4×2 plus drawbar

6×4 plus drawbar

Generally, the biggest four-wheeled trucks can weigh up to 16.26 tonnes, a rigid six-wheeler up to 24.4 tonnes, and a rigid eight-wheeler up to 30.5 tonnes. Most articulated trucks have at least four axles – two on the tractor and two on the semi-trailer. If these are far enough apart, the gross weight may be up to 32.5 tonnes, and if either the tractor or the semi-trailer has three axles then the gross weight can be 38 tonnes. Few drawbar trailers are owned in Britain because the top limit for a truck carrying a load itself and also hauling a trailer is only 32.5 tonnes.

All these are maximum weights only. There are many lighter trucks, built to suit the needs of different users, but they too must fit into weight categories.

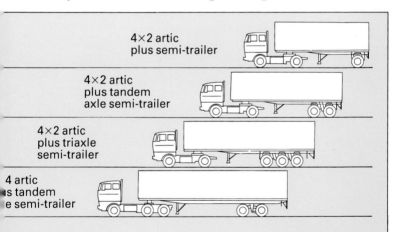

4×2 artic
plus semi-trailer

4×2 artic
plus tandem
axle semi-trailer

4×2 artic
plus triaxle
semi-trailer

4 artic
s tandem
e semi-trailer

COMMON VEHICLE FORMATS

These are some of the common wheel arrangements you will see on trucks today. The first number refers to the number of wheels; the second refers to the number of driven wheels.

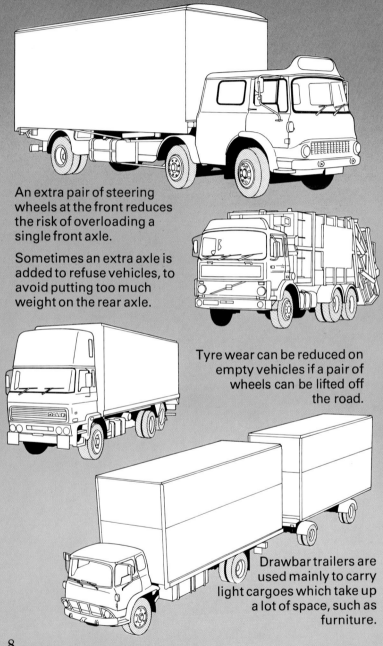

An extra pair of steering wheels at the front reduces the risk of overloading a single front axle.

Sometimes an extra axle is added to refuse vehicles, to avoid putting too much weight on the rear axle.

Tyre wear can be reduced on empty vehicles if a pair of wheels can be lifted off the road.

Drawbar trailers are used mainly to carry light cargoes which take up a lot of space, such as furniture.

8

Bodywork

Nearly all truck bodywork today is made of metal. Ordinary steel is cheap and strong, but must be painted to prevent rusting. Stainless steel is sometimes used for tankers – it is expensive and difficult to work, but it will stay shiny and bright. Aluminium alloys are lighter than steel, and do not need painting, but are more costly.

Plastics are used only for parts of bodies – for example, the roofs of vans. Because these materials are easy to clean, they are used for insulated vans too.

Wooden bodywork is rarely fitted to trucks these days. It is a long time since the usual way to build bodies was wooden framing held together with steel brackets, and wooden panelling.

The first motor trucks were built at the turn of the last century. They had simple flat platform bodies, and drivers became very skilful at covering their loads with canvas sheets called tarpaulins, roping them down so that cargoes would not be affected by bad weather. The first covered vans were hardly more than platforms over which a tent-like structure of canvas and framing (a 'tilt') was built.

Loads on flat platforms are protected with tarpaulins.

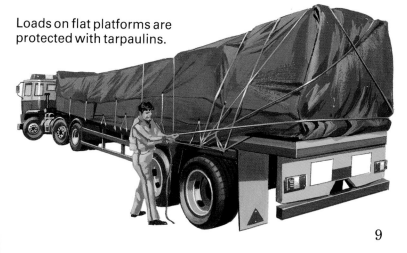

It soon became obvious that when a vehicle was used to carry one kind of freight, it would be better to provide it with specially tailored bodywork. Originally, for instance, petrol and paraffin were transported on flats in separate two-gallon cans, but when the quantities to be carried increased, tanker bodywork came into use.

As the years went by, it became possible to carry more and more kinds of goods in special tankers. Some of them are quite surprising – hot liquid sugar and chocolate, wine, cement, flour, and many kinds of chemicals.

The round-shaped steel tankers are very strong – far more so than most straight-sided trucks. But although they are ideal for carrying large quantities of liquid loads, they do have problems of their own. For example, if the tank is not filled to its limit, the weight of the

Petrol and oil are carried in special tankers, like the one shown above.

liquid surging around inside could cause the tanker to overbalance dangerously when it turned corners. Special compartments are therefore built inside the tank to divide up the load.

There is also the problem of getting goods in and out of the tanker. Not all cargoes are as free-running as milk or petrol, and sometimes pumps are needed to fill and empty the tank. Other goods, like tar and fats, need special heating coils to melt down the load to a liquid state at the unloading point.

Tankers are also used to carry some free-running solids, such as powdered flour and cement. This type of load needs to be mixed with air if it is to pour easily. Some tankers carrying this type of load can also be fitted with a tipping arrangement to help with the unloading.

Very strong tanks are needed to transport gas at high pressures.

Many straight-sided trucks are used to carry loose loads. Since tipping bodies were introduced, unloading cargoes such as sand or coal has become a very rapid job – certainly much quicker than shovelling by hand.

Tippers have been developed for carrying all kinds of goods. Most people think of them as being used only in the building industry, but many are at work carrying grain, plastics, and anything else that will discharge by tipping.

Although flats with their carefully-sheeted loads are still seen on the roads today, they have two big drawbacks. Firstly, cargoes are at the mercy of thieves

Fork-lift trucks help to speed up loading and unloading.

Tippers are a convenient way to load and unload sand and gravel.

and are only partly protected from bad weather. Secondly, it takes a long time to unwrap a load, fold the tarpaulins, coil the rope – and then sheet up the new cargo.

The answer was to let enclosed vans take over. More and more kinds of freight were made suitable for handling through van doorways, often using fork-lift trucks to fetch and carry. To speed up loading and unloading, many vans have curtain sides which can be pulled right back to open up their whole lengths. Others are fitted with platform lifts which raise and lower loads to pavement level.

With a platform lift one man can handle half-tonne loads.

A natural step forward was to develop insulated vans, and many are also used as very large refrigerators. They can carry not only foodstuffs, but other types of goods that must be kept cool. Most of these fridge vans can be recognized by the **compressor unit** mounted high up on the body front, or sometimes under the floor. Look for heavy seals and door bolts on all insulated vans.

International trucks crossing frontiers must be checked by Customs officers, to make sure that the cargo has not been touched since loading. Many trucks used on these types of journey use canvas tilts sewn down by a rope. This is threaded through many small eyelets and then sealed. It is the job of the Customs officers to check that the seals have not been tampered with.

International tilt bodies are sealed with ropes.

Fridge vans usually have a compressor on the body front.

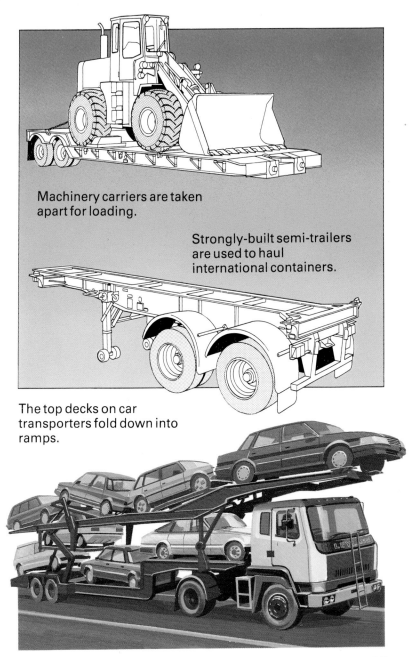

Machinery carriers are taken apart for loading.

Strongly-built semi-trailers are used to haul international containers.

The top decks on car transporters fold down into ramps.

Heavy Trucks

The biggest trucks are used to carry freight that is either heavy or bulky. They must be strongly built – yet their own weight has to be kept as low as possible, because the maximum allowed for such vehicles is the weight of vehicle and cargo added together. Most heavies are articulated: that is, a tractor part with engine and driver's cab supports the front end of a semi-trailer. The semi-trailer contains all of the cargo, and carries much of the weight. Other heavies have rigid **chassis**, and these are fitted with bodywork to carry their loads. A few rigids also haul drawbar trailers: this kind of trailer supports all of its contents, putting none of the weight on to the vehicle which tows it. In some countries, articulated trucks can be seen hauling additional drawbar trailers. This combination is called a double-bottom.

BEDFORD TM (British)
Bedford moved into heavy vehicle production with its TM family, which are built up from parts made by specialist manufacturers. The TM has been made in four- and six-wheeled forms, and as four- and six-wheeled tractors. Their cabs are made from standard parts: many are narrow, with steps over the front wheels, others as here are full width, and some are extended backwards to make space for a sleeping bunk.

DAF 3300 (Dutch)
The typical DAF is a big tractor running at up to 38 tonnes gross weight, usually four-wheeled but sometimes six-wheeled with two steering or two driving axles. The company also arranges its basic collection of engines, gearboxes, and axles to produce heavy four-, six-, and eight-wheeled rigid chassis for carrying loads.

DATE_____

NUMBER_____

Although the company used to be very successful, and many thousands of medium-weight Bedford trucks are in use all over the world, its American owners have decided to make no more of them for civilian buyers.

DATE_____

NUMBER_____

ERF (British)
Although ERF has standard designs, the company will build trucks to special order. Most, however, will look much the same. Not many two-axled rigids are made: most ERFs are tractors, with some rigid six- and eight-wheelers. Unusually the cab is made of plastics. This one is hauling a tanker used for carrying a fine powder: compressed air blows the load out, and tipping helps to speed up emptying.

DATE_____

NUMBER_____

FODEN (British)
Because they have traditionally been well made and costly, Foden products last a long time. Many six- and eight-wheelers of this general type are still in use, a common sight at road works and other big building projects where a high top speed is less important than toughness and an ability to get on and off sites with poor ground surfaces. Their striking-looking cabs were made in plastics.

DATE_____

NUMBER_____

IVECO-FIAT 190 (European)
Iveco is a company which includes the Italian Fiat, French Unic, and German Magirus-Deutz. It also controls Ford truck building in Europe. Vehicles bearing the Iveco name are often still recognizable as products of their original companies, but there is increasing use of the same sets of parts. Iveco makes all kinds of vehicles; articulated tractors from its Fiat heavy truck range are to be seen everywhere.

DATE_____

NUMBER_____

LEYLAND T45 (British)
Leyland is one company, but it used to be several separate ones. All its lorries are now part of one family in which a few types of engines, gearboxes, and axles are put together in several different arrangements. The standard 38-tonne Roadtrain tractor has four wheels. Cabs are also made from a limited number of parts: on smaller Leylands the cab is mounted lower; big ones have **filler panels** over the front wheels.

DATE_____

NUMBER_____

AEC MARSHAL (British)
This Ergomatic cab was once used on trucks sold as Leyland, AEC and Albion, and many of these older machines are still in use. They are quite different mechanically, and most of those left are Leylands. The 'tip and slide' body on this AEC is specially adapted to act as a storage bin for heavy scrap material.

DATE_____

NUMBER_____

LEYLAND REIVER (British)
Leyland used to produce two separate ranges of vehicles for users who needed low-weight trucks. These vehicles were very similar seen from the outside. They were made as four- and six-wheelers, and as articulated tractors: many of all types are still in use, working hard in all kinds of industries.

DATE_____

NUMBER_____

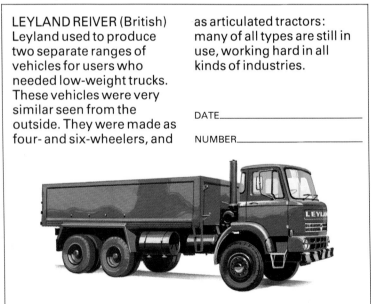

LEYLAND SCAMMELL ROUTEMAN (British)
Leyland still uses the Scammell name for some products, but on modern six- and eight-wheeled Constructor chassis the 'Scammell' badge is very small and low down on the cab front. These older Scammells are still commonly seen. Their cabs are made in plastics materials, and are quite unlike any other truck make.

DATE_____

NUMBER_____

MAN 20.321 (West German)
MAN has always made heavy duty trucks. While four-wheeled tractor units are the main product line, in common with most of its competitors, it also builds multi-axled tractors and rigids, including eight-wheeled tippers.

DATE_____

NUMBER_____

21

MERCEDES-BENZ 2033
(West German)

Some years ago, Mercedes-Benz decided that heavy commercial vehicles looked too 'aggressive', and so it spent enormous sums of money in designing and building the 'friendly' looking cabs it uses now. The company specializes in making tractors for maximum capacity articulated trucks, but in Britain the limit is only 38 tonnes gross weight – although almost all other countries allow higher limits.

SCANIA 141 (Swedish)

Scania makes most kinds of heavy commercial vehicles. Many are four-wheeled tractors, but look carefully at Scania tractors or rigids with six wheels. Quite often only the second axle is driven, and the rearmost one can be lifted so that its wheels are clear of the ground. This can help in two ways – it reduces tyre wear, and puts more weight on the driving wheels to give better grip.

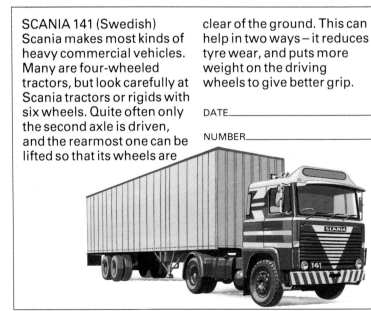

SEDDON-ATKINSON 401
(British)
This company was once two separate firms, and 'Atkinson' heavy lorries are still frequently seen on the roads. There are fewer 'Seddons', which were lighter, left in service. Most of the modern heavies will have a distinctive 'A' in a circle badge on their grilles.

DATE_____

NUMBER_____

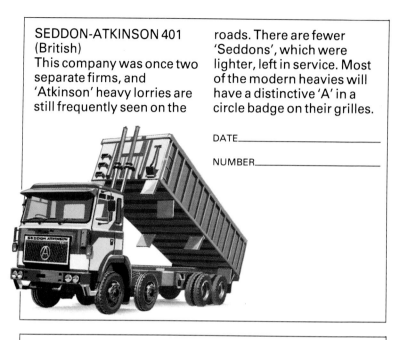

VOLVO F12 (Swedish)
Volvo trucks are well made, and so many of the older F86 and F88 models are still running – the latter unmistakeable with their high square cabs. For long distance international work where drivers live in their vehicles Volvo produces special tractors which have cabs that are fitted out like caravans.

DATE_____

NUMBER_____

23

Medium Trucks

For many purposes, medium-sized four-wheeled trucks are more convenient than bigger vehicles. It may be that they have to work in busy towns, where traffic makes larger trucks a problem. And in some cases it can be better for two trucks to make one delivery each rather than have one big vehicle handling the deliveries. Although medium-weights are well made, most will not be of the same high quality as the heaviest kinds of vehicles. Quite often medium-weight chassis are used as a base frame on which other vehicle parts can be mounted, to make articulated trucks that can manage gross weights of 24 tonnes or more. However, a driver holding a driving licence for medium-weight trucks may not drive anything bigger than four wheels or with a gross weight of more than 16.2 tonnes.

BEDFORD TL (British)
Bedford specialized in mass-producing low-priced light and medium weight trucks. They all share the same cab design, but a way of recognizing big TLs from small ones is by their different-sized wheels.

Bedfords are used to carry goods for every kind of industry, and are much missed by users who once bought nothing else.

DATE_____

NUMBER_____

BEDFORD TK (British)

The Bedford TK was made in thousands, and many are in use. Although the cab extends behind the driver it is not a sleeper: instead, it covers the engine. This TK is equipped to carry **swop bodies**, which can be loaded or emptied while the chassis is kept busy making deliveries.

DATE_____

NUMBER_____

BEDFORD VANPLAN (British)

Furniture removers need very large, but light, box vans and their distinctive vehicles are often seen. Many have Bedford chassis, but other makes are also used, and unless the wheel hubs are recognized, identification can be difficult.

DATE_____

NUMBER_____

DAF FA2100 (Dutch)

Most medium-sized trucks are also medium-priced, but some users are willing to pay more for 'premium' vehicles, made to the very high standards of heavy tractors. One of these is the DAF FA2100, which could work at 18 tonnes gross weight. In Britain, though, it is limited to 16.2 tonnes, so it can never be overloaded and strained. The cab roof **air deflector** helps to reduce fuel consumption.

DATE_____

NUMBER_____

DODGE G16 COMMANDO (British)

The French company Renault bought the Dodge factory in Britain, but still makes some of the old Dodge designs. Like many British products they are assembled from parts bought in from specialist suppliers. Most Commandos are four-wheeled rigids. Its low cost makes it a favourite among local authority buyers, who use it for refuse collectors, fire appliances, and other special purposes. This vehicle has a crew cab to carry a team of workmen, and mounted on its back is a device that bores holes in the ground to receive electricity supply poles.

DATE_____

NUMBER_____

ERF (British)
Because their maximum weight limit of 16.2 tonnes gross has not been altered for many years, some quite old four-wheelers are still to be seen in use. If, that is, they were well made in the first place. ERFs are well made, and unlike nearly all their rivals the cabs are made in plastics materials. This has made it possible to change the designs quite frequently. They are always eye-catching.

DATE_____

NUMBER_____

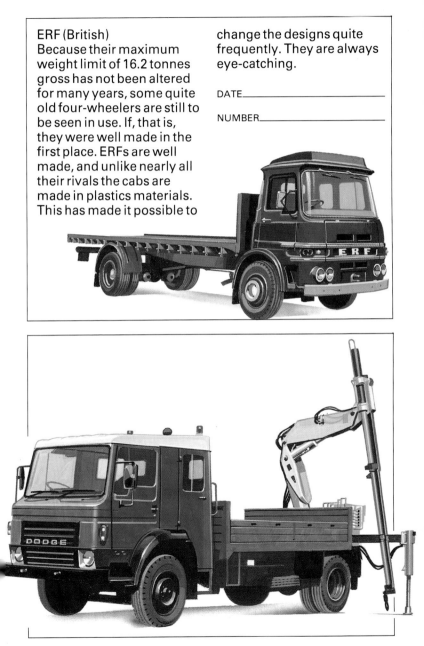

FORD CARGO 1115 (British)
There is an enormous number of different chassis within the Ford Cargo range of vehicles, because Ford is another maker which tries to meet every kind of need. Most Cargoes are medium-weight four-wheelers fitted with almost any imaginable kind of bodywork. This variety means Cargoes are well suited to delivery work, where the needs of the user vary a great deal.

DATE_____

NUMBER_____

FORD D-SERIES (British)
The D-series, like the Cargo which replaced it, was made in many different forms including articulateds and rigid six-wheelers. Little ones delivered bread for bakers; big ones carried concrete for builders. This tipper hauled coal. So many were made in this series that they will be a common sight for years to come.

DATE_____

NUMBER_____

HESTAIR-DENNIS DELTA
(British)

Dennis was once one of the biggest makers of commercial vehicles in Britain. Now it builds buses, fire appliances – and just a few four-wheeled trucks. For vehicles of their size they have unusually large and square cabs, set low down over the front wheels: these cabs are much the same as those used on the fire appliances, where space is needed to carry several people and their equipment.

DATE_____

NUMBER_____

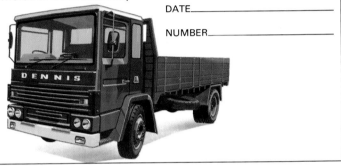

LEYLAND FREIGHTER 1314
(British)

Freighters and the similar-looking Cruiser articulated tractors, like all the modern Leylands, are fitted with cabs made from a very few parts, so it can be difficult to recognize individual models at a glance. But they do have their model numbers on plates just beneath the door locks. One minor detail is the flat panel under the windscreen of medium weights: the big Roadtrain has slots in this panel.

DATE_____

NUMBER_____

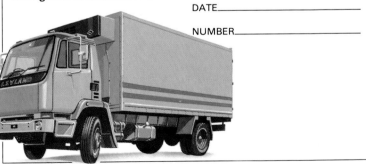

LEYLAND BOXER (British)
Until the present Freighters and Cruisers were introduced, Leyland had several quite separate ranges of trucks. One range had Scottish names – Reiver and Clydesdale – while this Boxer was part of a family of dogs. They all shared similar cab designs. These models are still a common sight on the roads today.

DATE_____

NUMBER_____

MAN-VW 10.136 (West German)
When MAN and VW got together the partners had a range of heavy trucks and a range of light ones – but nothing in between. So they set to work and introduced the MT, which bridges the gap. Several kinds of MT are made, using MAN engines and VW transmissions: they all have comparatively small wheels, which makes them easier to load and unload.

DATE_____

NUMBER_____

SEDDON-ATKINSON 201
(British)
Unlike many premium four-wheelers used in Britain, which could carry much more if they were allowed to, the 201 is designed to take loads of just 16.26 tonnes. It is, therefore, no heavier than it needs to be. Keeping the standard Seddon-Atkinson cab low on the chassis is one way of saving some weight: it has been done by leaving out the filler piece fitted over the front wheels of the big 401 trucks.

DATE_____

NUMBER_____

Light Trucks

If the gross weight of a truck and its cargo can be kept to not more than 7.5 tonnes then its driver needs no special driving licence. This is the main reason that so many light vehicles are made and used. Almost all of them belong to families which also include much larger vehicles, and there is usually a family resemblance too – particularly in the cabs. These vehicles are designed in such a way that almost any kind of bodywork can be fitted, to meet the needs of different kinds of users. Lightweights are always worked hard in difficult conditions, and so they do not have long life spans. Every kind of trade uses them, but most spend their time on short journeys. It is useful for them to have small wheels, so that drivers can climb in and out of the cabs more easily during their many stops.

DODGE 50-SERIES (British) The 50-series was designed when Dodge belonged to Chrysler. Now the company is owned by Renault, and vehicles carry the Renault badge on the front. The factory-made vans are square and old-fashioned in appearance, but all kinds of bodywork is mounted on these chassis.

DATE_____

NUMBER_____

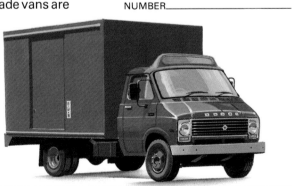

FORD CARGO 0811 (British)
Among the smaller members of the huge family of Cargoes is the 0811. The only sure way of recognizing any of them is to look at the model number shown in the cab side window. The body on this example is unusual because it has roller shutters. Most users now prefer to fit curtain sides, which are less likely to be damaged.

DATE_____

NUMBER_____

IVECO 79.14 (Italian)
There is a factory-built van on the 79.14 chassis, and a side loading door – but most of these vehicles are sold as chassis-cabs to outside specialists who will build the body. This one is a general purpose box, with a tailgate lift to make loading and unloading easier. Aluminium mouldings protect the large one-piece side panels from scrapes. Three windscreen wipers is an unusual detail.

DATE_____

NUMBER_____

LEYLAND TERRIER (British)
The Terrier was the smallest member of the 'dog' range of Leyland trucks. It shared the cab design of the larger ones, and so the arch over the wheels is too big for the Terrier's much smaller ones. There was no built-in van version: all the chassis had their bodies built by outside builders. Although no longer made, Terriers will be a common sight for a long while yet.

DATE_____

NUMBER_____

LEYLAND ROADRUNNER 8.12 (British)
Roadrunner replaced Terrier, and it is the smallest model in a range of Leyland trucks that extends up to the 65-tonnes Roadtrain. This one is unusual in having a sleeper extension fitted to the cabs. Any Roadrunner can be instantly recognized by its extra, lower, windscreen: this gives the driver a good view of the kerb.

DATE_____

NUMBER_____

MAN-VW MT 8.90 (West German)
This tipper is intended to be used only up to the 7.5 tonnes gross weight limit. Look at the strong framework under the tipping body and on the sides, and see also how the chassis frame is stiffened to resist the heavy twisting stresses that all tippers have to survive.

DATE_____

NUMBER_____

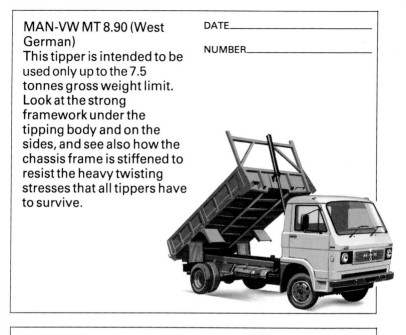

MERCEDES-BENZ 814 (West German)
The over-large wheelarch shows that the 814 cab is also used in much the same form on larger vehicles. This van has three air-deflectors – one on the cab roof, and one each side of the front grille. The box van body is a plain structure suitable for many trades.

DATE_____

NUMBER_____

Panel Vans

For general purpose fetching and carrying, panel vans are invaluable. Unlike the larger kinds of vehicles these vans are made in much the same way as motor cars, and in similar factories. They get their name because most (such as the Bedford CF2 shown below) are made as vans with pressed steel panelling: the driving position is made as part of the bodywork space. However, some are turned out as small trucks, with separate enclosed cabs and chassis frames on which special bodywork can be fitted. The original Ford Transit shown opposite is typical of this type of van. All of these vehicles can expect to be badly treated and they wear out quite quickly, but because it is very expensive indeed to set up factories to make them the designs do not change much over many years.

BEDFORD CF2 (British)
Bedford CFs have been made for many years, and are instantly recognizable by the rounded body shape and the stubby little bonnet. Although they are assembled from a limited range of components there is plenty of variety in the vans: short, long, and even longer bodies; single or twin rear wheels; petrol or diesel engines; and chassis-cab versions for fitting with non-standard bodies.

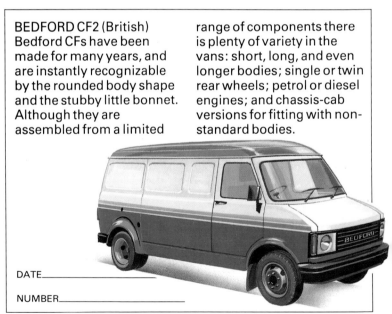

DATE_____

NUMBER_____

FORD TRANSIT (British)
The original Ford Transit was made for very many years and in very many forms. Similar body parts were used for all models in its range, from small to large. Transit chassis-cabs have been fitted with all kinds of bodywork. This high capacity van is suitable for all kinds of trades, from light furniture removals to parcels or laundry deliveries.

DATE_____

NUMBER_____

FORD TRANSIT (British)
When the time finally came to design a new Transit, Ford adopted the sloping front that is fashionable with some European makers. Despite the **streamlined** front the rest of the standard panel van bodies are actually more square than the earlier ones. This detail increases the amount of useful load space.

DATE_____

NUMBER_____

IVECO DAILY 35.8 (Italian)
Iveco makes a large range of panel vans and related chassis-cabs, and the Daily is typical of the middle-sized ones. This version has a gross weight capacity of 3.5 tonnes, so it falls just inside one of the legal categories of commercial vehicles. It is of standard height: there is also a high-roofed model.

DATE_____

NUMBER_____

NISSAN CABSTAR (Japanese)
The Nissan vans and related vehicles – like this drop-side pick-up – are typical of many models produced by several Japanese makers. Even the appearances of these competing makes are similar. A strong selling point with all these vehicles is that they have 'car-style' fittings and trim.

DATE_____

NUMBER_____

SUZUKI SUPER-CARRY (Japanese)

This micro van has a carrying capacity of 650 kg. The Suzuki is unusual because it competes with identical vehicles which are sold with 'Bedford Rascal' labels: the companies are associated through General Motors of America.

DATE_____

NUMBER_____

VOLKSWAGEN LT28 (West German)

The LT-series is the larger of two distinct families of VW panel vans, and like most vehicles of its kind, the engine is at the front, under the cab seats. The LT28 is made in either of two body lengths, and a high roof can be supplied.

DATE_____

NUMBER_____

Car-derived Vans

If certain alterations are made to ordinary motor cars
they can be adapted for carrying small quantities of
goods. The most difficult and expensive part to change is
the bodywork, and on most designs it can be seen that the
designers have tried to alter as little as possible – in some
cases, even pressed metal 'windows' are used in place of
glass. Another difficulty is that most modern cars do not
have a separate chassis frame, so if an open or special
van body is going to be fitted then a chassis has to be
provided. Fortunately, just a few changes are needed to
adapt the mechanical parts of ordinary motor cars for
vehicles used for carrying goods.

Because car-derived vans are so similar to the cars
they are based on, each model is suitable for personal use
as well as goods transport.

AUSTIN ROVER METRO 310
(British)
Metro vans have almost the
same bodywork as Metro
cars, but the inside is altered
to give a flat floor at the
back, and at the same time
as much space as possible.
At the front, the driving
compartments are also very
much the same as the cars.
The model number comes
from its carrying capacity of
310 kg.

DATE_____

NUMBER_____

BEDFORD ASTRAMAX 365L (British)

Modern cars have low roof lines, so it can be difficult to make the inside of a car-derived van body high enough to be useful. In adapting the Vauxhall Astra car for commercial use, Bedford kept all of the car front end: the new body roof was made higher, and the sides were pushed out to make a kind of streamlined box. The result looks quite unlike most other small vans, and the Astramax can be recognized at once.

DATE_____

NUMBER_____

BEDFORD KB 26 (Japanese–British)

Pickups of this kind have become very popular, and many of them are sold for use as private cars as much as for business work. Japanese makers hold a great deal of the market, so instead of designing a pick-up of its own, Bedford asked its Isuzu associate to provide a suitable vehicle. The results are sold as Bedfords. This is a two-wheel drive KB; there is a similar-looking model which has all-wheel drive.

DATE_____

NUMBER_____

FORD FIESTA (British)
The Fiesta is another of the 'super mini' cars to which only minor changes have to be made to turn it into a generally useful light van. As in others of its kind, the payload (about 400 kg in the Fiesta) is placed in the best position – over the rear wheels. In common with many small cars, the Fiesta has a lift-up hatchback rear door, which gives some protection while loading in the rain.

DATE⎯⎯⎯⎯⎯⎯⎯⎯⎯⎯⎯⎯

NUMBER⎯⎯⎯⎯⎯⎯⎯⎯⎯

FORD ESCORT (British)
Escort is a name that has been used by Ford on cars and vans for many years, but while older ones drive through the rear wheels the modern Escorts have front-wheel drive. Although front-end panelling is shared by vans and cars, the vans are designed so that their bodywork does not look like an afterthought: the roof is high enough to allow double hinged doors at the back. Notice the narrow window behind each side door.

DATE⎯⎯⎯⎯⎯⎯⎯⎯⎯⎯⎯⎯

NUMBER⎯⎯⎯⎯⎯⎯⎯⎯⎯

FIAT FIORINO (Italian)
The makers of the Fiorino accept the fact that cars are not really high enough to carry real cargoes – and so they have put a large square box behind the cab, and fitted it with side-hinged doors that open right back to make loading and unloading as easy as possible. Carrying capacity is 520 kg. There is also a roof rack fitted over the cab.

DATE_____

NUMBER_____

VOLKSWAGEN POLO (West German)
In producing a van version of its little polo hatchback car, VW was helped considerably by its squared-off rear – most of the super minis have a fairly steep slope at the back, and this reduces the amount of internal space.

DATE_____

NUMBER_____

Special Trucks

Nearly all 'special' trucks are really just ordinary ones that have been altered to meet a specific need. Usually, changes are made to the engine and gearbox combinations, or to the road springs, and sometimes an axle will be added or replaced by a heavier duty one. Often a chassis frame will be made stronger to meet some need, and for some jobs it may have to be lengthened, or shortened. Perhaps only the size of the tyres will be changed. Usually therefore the only specials that can be easily recognized from the roadside are those which carry unusual kinds of bodywork or superstructure. As well as the specials shown here, remember to look out for the well-known emergency trucks, such as fire engines and crash tenders. Nearly all special-purpose trucks are rigids: few have trailers or semi-trailers.

GULLY AND CESSPOOL EMPTIER

Skip wagons are quite common. They always have specially strengthened chassis frames, and strong legs at the back which are lowered to take the strain off the rear tyres while loads are being lifted. But in addition to skips they can carry other things: this one has a tank that is used to empty sewage tanks and roadside gullies.

DATE_____

NUMBER_____

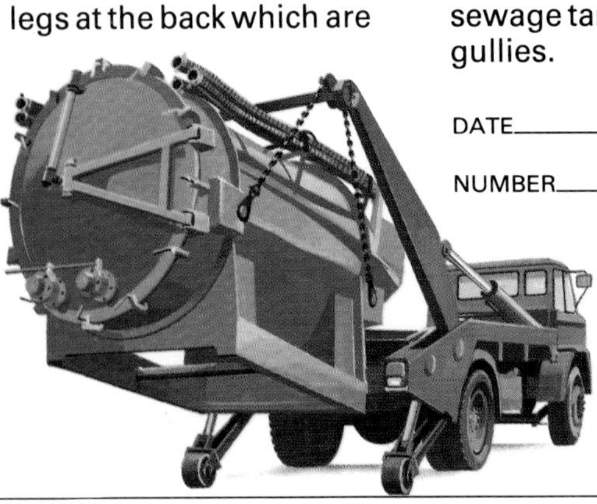

HYDRAULIC WORK PLATFORM

The usefulness of these machines is evident to anyone who has watched one being used for cleaning tall street lights or for work under bridges. Most are mounted on strengthened truck chassis, which have stabilizing legs added. This one is built onto an ordinary panel van which has had side stabilizers fitted.

DATE_____

NUMBER_____

TWIN-BOOM RECOVERY VEHICLE

Recovery units are used to rescue other vehicles which have crashed or broken down in service, and they are made very strongly indeed. The twin-boom is a kind of powerful crane, which easily pulls loaded heavy trucks up motorway embankments and out of rivers, and across wide fields. They can of course also tow any heavy vehicle on ordinary roads.

DATE_____

NUMBER_____

UNDER-REACH RECOVERY VEHICLE

The under-reach has a strong arm which can be made to stick out at the back. This arm is long enough to reach under the axles of coaches, and strong enough to raise them off the road. In this way the casualty vehicle can be safely towed away with no risk of crane ropes causing damage to its panels. The under-reach can work quickly, so it is ideal for moving any heavy vehicle which breaks down on busy roads.

DATE_____

NUMBER_____

SPECTACLE LIFT RECOVERY VEHICLE

Because modern cars and light vans have easily-damaged panels at their fronts and backs, it is better to lift them by the wheels. One way of moving them safely when they break down is by using a spectacle lift recovery unit. This has an arm at the back and a pair of frames – 'spectacles' – which fit round a pair of wheels on the casualty vehicle. An advantage is that only one man is needed to bring in a breakdown.

DATE_____

NUMBER_____

ROADSWEEPER
Two main kinds of roadsweeper are made, with either rotating brushes or vacuum cleaners. Each is best at its own kind of work – vacuum cleaners are good with leaves; brushes are better with stones. Most sweepers have left-hand drive, so that the drivers can see the kerb. But for cleaning both sides of one-way streets some machines are fitted with two steering wheels and two sets of controls.

DATE_____

NUMBER_____

MILITARY TRANSPORT
Armies have special transport needs, and although several makes of vehicle are used, they look much the same. Because they must be able to carry loads at high speeds over rough country the trucks are big and tough, and all their wheels are driven. Good ground clearance is needed, so bodies and cabs are mounted high. Look for the heavy shield under the front. This protects the underside from rocks and tree stumps.

DATE_____

NUMBER_____

Index